Fact Finders®

ADVENTURES ON THE AMERICAN FRONTIER

CONNECTING THE COASTS

THE RACE TO BUILD THE TRANSCONTINENTAL RAILROAD

BY NORMA LEWIS

Consultant:
Walter R. Borneman
Author and American Historian

CAPSTONE PRESS
a capstone imprint

Fact Finders are published by Capstone Press,
1710 Roe Crest Drive, North Mankato, Minnesota 56003
www.capstonepub.com

LIBRARY OF CONGRESS CATALOGING-IN-PUBLICATION DATA
Lewis, Norma, 1940–
Connecting the coasts : the race to build the transcontinental railroad / by Norma Lewis.
pages cm.—(Fact finders. Adventures on the American frontier)
Summary: "Examines the Transcontinental Railroad by discussing why it was needed and the immediate and lasting effects it had on the nation as well as the people and places involved."—Provided by publisher.
Audience: Ages 8–12.
Audience: Grades 4–6.
Includes bibliographical references and index.
ISBN 978-1-4914-0186-6 (library binding)
ISBN 978-1-4914-0191-0 (paperback)
ISBN 978-1-4914-0195-8 (ebook PDF)
1. Union Pacific Railroad Company—History—Juvenile literature. 2. Central Pacific Railroad Company—
TF25.P23L49 2015
385.0973—dc239   2014007816

EDITORIAL CREDITS
Jennifer Huston, editor; Sarah Bennett, series designer; Kazuko Collins, layout artist;
Wanda Winch, media researcher; Tori Abraham, production specialist

PHOTO CREDITS
The Bridgeman Art Library: Peter Newark American Pictures, 14; Bruce Cooper Collection of North American Railroadana, 10, 12, 16, 17, 18 (top), 27; Capstone: 8, 25 (map); Corbis, 4, Bettmann, 15, 19 (left); Courtesy Scotts Bluff National Monument: William Henry Jackson, 9; CriaImages.com: Jay Robert Nash Collection, 21; Getty Images: George Eastman House/Mora, 20 (bottom), Kean Collection, 18 (b), MPI, cover; Library of Congress: Prints and Photographs Division, 11, 19 (right), 29; Nebraska State Historical Society, 20 (top), Shutterstock: 06photo, book page bkgrnd, homey design, leather design, Itana, sunburst design, ixer, 1 (banner), LongQuattro, 8, 25 (compass), Miljoe, 7 (top right), Picsfive, parchment paper design; SuperStock: SuperStock, 26; The Powder Monkeys, Cape Horn, 1865, ©Mian Situ, licensed by The Greenwich Workshop, Inc. www.greenwichworkshop.com, 5, Ten Miles in One Day, Victory Camp, Utah, April 28, 1869, ©Mian Situ, licensed by The Greenwich Workshop, Inc. www.greenwichworkshop.com, 23; Union Pacific Railroad Museum, 13; Washington State Historical Society: University of Washington Libraries, 6–7

PRIMARY SOURCE BIBLIOGRAPHY
Page 19—"Transcontinental Railroad." *American Experience*. Directed by Mark Zwonitzer and Michael Chin.
        2003. www.pbs.org/wgbh/americanexperience/features/general-article/tcrr-uprr/
Page 27—Williams, John Hoyt. *A Great and Shining Road: The Epic Story of the Transcontinental Railroad.*
        New York: Times Books, 1988.

Printed in the United States of America in Stevens Point, Wisconsin.
032014   008092WZF14

TABLE OF CONTENTS

CHAPTER 1

CONNECTING AMERICA FROM COAST TO COAST

The men labored all day, doing the same thing they did the day before, and would do again the next. Day after day they blasted tunnels through the solid granite of the mountains. For hours they bored 15-foot (4.6-meter) holes in the rock. Their backs ached from swinging sledgehammers. Their hands throbbed from sharpening drills. Even though it was cold, their shirts were drenched with sweat.

Blasting holes through the mountains was very dangerous work.

Chinese laborers dangled over the side of mountains to bore holes in the rock.

The workers were numb with fatigue, but they still had to do the most dangerous job of all. First they crammed the holes full of black gunpowder. Then carefully—oh so carefully—they stuck the fuse in, lit it, … and ran! Would luck be on their side? Would they be able to scramble to safety before the explosion? They would soon find out.

Pushing the Boundaries

In 1803 President Thomas Jefferson's **Louisiana Purchase** doubled the country's size. A year later he sent Meriwether Lewis and William Clark to explore this unknown territory. Their adventure across the country took them all the way to the Pacific Ocean.

Lewis and Clark befriended many American Indian tribes on their journey across America.

After Lewis and Clark's journey, fur traders and trappers started exploring the western part of the country more. There were no roads back then, but the trappers eventually established trails. One became known as the Oregon Trail because it went all the way from Missouri to Oregon. Another trail branched off and led to California. For many years, these trails were the quickest ways to travel to the western part of the country.

MANIFEST DESTINY

Some people believed in "Manifest Destiny"—that it was the right of all Americans to occupy all the land between the Atlantic and Pacific Oceans. Not everyone agreed. The American Indians knew that westward expansion would disturb the buffalo on their hunting grounds. They relied on buffalo for food and for making clothing, tepees, and tools.

Louisiana Purchase—an 1803 deal with France in which the United States bought land that would eventually become parts of 15 states

There Must Be an Easier Way

In the early 1800s, traveling from coast to coast was difficult and dangerous. It took up to 10 weeks to get from New York to San Francisco by stagecoach. The same trip could take eight months by horse and wagon. These vehicles bumped over rocks, splashed through streams, and plodded up steep mountain passes. It was a long and tiring journey, and many people died along the way.

Sailing took five to six months. Travelers sailed down the Atlantic coast to Cape Horn on the southern tip of South America. From there they went up the Pacific coast to San Francisco. Choppy seas made passengers seasick. Heavy winds blew ships off course and many crashed on the rocky shores.

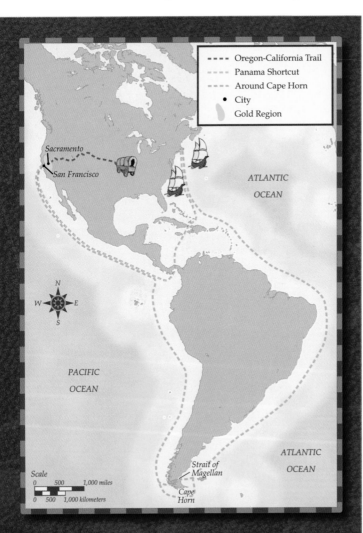

- - - Oregon-California Trail
- - - Panama Shortcut
- - - Around Cape Horn
• City
  Gold Region

Sacramento
San Francisco

ATLANTIC OCEAN

N
W E
S

PACIFIC OCEAN

ATLANTIC OCEAN

Scale
0   500   1,000 miles
0   500   1,000 kilometers

Strait of Magellan

Cape Horn

Traveling across the country in the early 1800s was a long, dangerous, and uncomfortable journey.

Others sailed down the Atlantic coast and crossed the **Isthmus** of Panama to the Pacific. This route took up to five months and could be just as deadly. Travelers roasted in the tropical heat, as biting, buzzing insects tormented them. Many died of **malaria** or **yellow fever**.

Because more and more families were packing up and moving west, a better route was needed. But almost all railroads were on the east side of the Mississippi River. It was time for a transcontinental railroad that linked the eastern United States with the rapidly expanding west.

isthmus—a narrow strip of land that has water on both sides and connects two larger sections of land
malaria—a serious disease that people get from mosquito bites; malaria causes high fever, chills, and sometimes death
yellow fever—an illness that can cause high fever, chills, nausea, kidney and liver failure; liver failure causes the skin to become yellow, giving the disease its name

Railroad Fever

In the mid-1850s, a civil engineer named Theodore Judah thought a railroad could be built through the Sierra Nevada mountains. He believed that tunnels could be blasted through the mountains and trains could steam through them. Most people called him "Crazy Judah" because they thought his idea was absolutely impossible.

At first he failed to convince Congress that the railroad could (and should) be built. But by 1860, Congress was on the brink of approving the project. However, the northern and southern states could not agree on the railroad's route. And both sides refused to budge.

That issue no longer mattered when South Carolina **seceded** from the Union in December 1860. When other southern states followed, they formed their own country called the Confederate States of America. With no one opposing them, the northern congressmen voted for the railroad. On July 1, 1862, President Abraham Lincoln signed the Pacific Railway Act. By doing so, Lincoln gave his stamp of approval for the construction of a transcontinental railroad.

Theodore Judah

secede—to formally withdraw from a group or an organization, often to form another organization

The Sierra Nevadas were one of the biggest obstacles to building a railroad from coast to coast.

The act stated that two companies would build the railroad. The Central Pacific Railroad Company would start laying track in Sacramento, California. The Union Pacific Railroad Company would start in Omaha, Nebraska. It was still undecided where the tracks would come together. From the start, the two companies competed to see who could work the fastest and lay the most track.

✺ FUN FACT ✺

On May 20, 1862, President Lincoln signed the Homestead Act into law. This law gave people—including freed slaves and women—land out west at little or no cost. The law made it much easier to settle in the West.

EAST FROM SACRAMENTO: THE CENTRAL PACIFIC

By the time Lincoln signed the railroad act, Judah had convinced four wealthy businessmen to form the Central Pacific Railroad Company. Leland Stanford, Collis Huntington, Mark Hopkins, and Charles Crocker were known as the Big Four. James Strobridge was hired to supervise the workers. Judah would have been the chief engineer, but he died of yellow fever after crossing the Isthmus of Panama.

Leland Stanford

Collis Huntington

Mark Hopkins

Charles Crocker

The government paid the railroad companies $16,000 for each mile (1.6 kilometers) of track laid in flat areas. They received $48,000 per mile (1.6 km) when blasting tunnels through mountains. Out of that, the companies had to pay for equipment and supplies, along with food and living quarters for the workers. The workers each received about $2 to $3 a day, which doesn't sound like much. But it was much more than they would have earned elsewhere.

Good Help Is Hard to Find

The Central Pacific broke ground in Sacramento on January 8, 1863. But due to money problems, the first rails weren't laid until October 26 of that year.

From the start, Strobridge had problems keeping workers. The Central Pacific needed about 10,000 men. But not all men were strong enough for the brutal job of laying track.

Laying railroad track was tiresome, backbreaking labor.

After the ground was prepared, 14 to 19 **railroad ties** were laid for every length of rail (one rail on each side). The wooden ties were about 8 feet (2.4 meters) long and weighed about 175 pounds (79 kilograms) each. They were placed width-wise below the iron rails, which were about 30 feet (9.1 m) long and weighed about 600 pounds (272 kg). It took 10 men (five on each side) to lay the iron rails. This meant that all together, the laborers lifted about 673,000 pounds (305,268 kg) for every mile of track laid. That's about the same as lifting 135 pickup trucks!

Crocker suggested hiring Chinese **immigrants**, but Strobridge thought they couldn't do the work. When Crocker reminded him that the Chinese had built the Great Wall of China, he agreed to try 50 men. They worked so hard that he hired thousands more. At one time, 80 percent of the men working on the Central Pacific tracks were Chinese.

Unfortunately racism ruled. Although the Chinese workers excelled in everything, they were only paid about half what the white men earned. Still, some of the white men teased them and called them names.

Boom!

In September 1865, the Central Pacific began the biggest challenge of the entire project—blasting tunnels through the Sierra Nevada mountains. It was mostly Chinese workers who bored holes into the rock and filled them with explosives. Then they risked their lives to light a fuse and run for cover.

railroad tie—a rectangular, wooden support for the rails in railroad tracks
immigrant—a person who moves from one country to live permanently in another

Challenges and Hardships

Conditions worsened when the workers reached the ridge nicknamed Cape Horn. There they were lucky if they progressed a foot a day. Tunneling through this mountain proved to be impossible, but there was another option. Rather than blowing a hole *into* the mountain, they could blast granite away from *the side* of the mountain. The track would be placed on the ledge that formed as a result.

A Chinese foreman suggested lowering workmen to the blasting site in large baskets. Desperation forced Strobridge to give it a try. He ordered reeds from San Francisco, and the Chinese workers wove them into baskets.

Soon they were back on the job. But now they did it hanging over the side of the mountain in baskets dangling from ropes. The baskets swayed in the high winds, and if the rope failed, the man in the basket would plunge into the river below. After lighting the fuse, the workers had only a few seconds to be pulled up to safety.

James Strobridge

ೲ FUN FACT ೲ

James Strobridge was a tough boss. He proved it one day in a tunnel when a blast of dynamite shot a piece of granite into his eye. He yanked it out, and kept shouting orders at his workers. He later lost the eye.

Not all of them made it. It is estimated that several hundred men died during construction of the transcontinental railroad. Those who survived faced danger every day.

Explosions and avalanches caused most of the deaths during construction of the Central Pacific. One avalanche killed 20 Chinese workers. Their bodies weren't found until the following spring. Others died from the blazing summer heat or the bone-chilling winter temperatures.

Heavy rain in the fall of 1865 stopped work when mudslides and fallen rocks blocked supply roads. Then in February 1866, a blizzard left snowdrifts as high as 60 feet (18 m). Digging out took days. But inch by inch, mile by mile, the Central Pacific Railroad crawled further east.

#

WEST FROM OMAHA: THE UNION PACIFIC

Thomas Durant

Grenville Dodge

Groundbreaking for the Union Pacific took place in Omaha, Nebraska, on December 2, 1863. But due to the Civil War and other delays, work didn't begin until July 1865—three months after President Lincoln was killed.

Thomas Durant headed the Union Pacific. He named former Civil War Major General Grenville Dodge as chief engineer.

The Union Pacific hired approximately 8,000 workers. Most were Irish and German immigrants. About 2,000 of the men laid railroad ties and track. The others worked as supervisors, blacksmiths, surveyors, carpenters, sawmill operators, and cooks.

"I've Been Working on the Railroad ..."

Everything the men needed—housing, food, materials, and so on—was kept on railcars on the finished tracks. As work progressed, railcars followed along and moved supplies. The men rarely bathed, and one worker later reported, "to tell the truth we were troubled by cooties." Cramped, dirty living conditions led to many deaths during construction of the railroad.

Trouble dogged the Union Pacific workers from the start. They encountered dust storms, blazing heat, swarming insects, snowstorms, and everything in between. People looking to make money quickly set up temporary towns along the way. There it was easy for workers to get into trouble drinking, gambling, and fighting with each other.

BRIGHAM YOUNG

In 1847 Brigham Young led members of the Church of Jesus Christ of Latter-day Saints (also called Mormons) to Salt Lake City, Utah. Young had always supported the railroad. He needed it to bring new Mormons to Utah. He bought **bonds** to help fund the Union Pacific. With his encouragement, more than 1,000 young Mormons went to work on the railroad.

bond—a paper that shows a person has loaned money to a company or government and will receive a larger amount in return

19

The workers also had trouble getting the timber they needed for railroad ties and **trestles**. Cottonwoods were plentiful, but the wood was too soft. Anything made of cottonwood would have to be replaced in two or three years. Forests in the upper Midwest could also provide timber, but floating logs down rivers to the remote sites cost too much.

Durant was under pressure to get the job done, so he took a chance. He had men build sawmills and cut cottonwood logs. Then they were hardened in a machine called a "burnettizer." Teams of oxen and horses then moved the lumber to where it was needed. That turned out to be a costly mistake. The burnettizer didn't work, and some of the cottonwood had to be replaced before the entire railroad was even complete.

༄ FUN FACT ༄

"Buffalo Bill" Cody earned his nickname when he bragged about shooting more than 4,000 buffalo in an 18-month period. Hunters like him helped speed up the near-extinction of the animals.

Costs of the American Dream

The workers also faced brutal attacks from American Indians. They were enraged when the railroad hired marksmen to kill buffalo to prevent them from getting in the way of construction.

In addition the American Indians no longer trusted the government to treat them fairly. The treaties the U.S. government had made with them had been broken. They were angry and hungry because they never received the money promised to them.

Enormous herds of buffalo sometimes blocked work on the railroad for hours.

trestle—a framework that holds up a railroad bridge
handcar—a small, four-wheeled railroad car operated by hand

CHAPTER 4

THE TEN-MILE DAY

Six years after construction began, the competition between the two railroads was still going strong. Coming in second in a field of two was unacceptable, and some workers took the competition too far. When the tracks were close to meeting, jealousy between the Chinese and Irish workers drove them to **sabotage** each other. They stole each other's supplies and set off their explosives.

Ten Miles? When Pigs Fly!

From the start, each railroad tried to outdo the other. Durant's Union Pacific had laid a record 6 miles (9.7 km) of track in a single day. Crocker's men rose to the challenge and laid 7 miles (11.3 km). Then in October 1868, Durant's team reclaimed the record with 7.5 miles (12.1 km).

As a result, Crocker boasted that the Central Pacific could lay 10 miles (16.1 km) of track in a single day. Durant bet him $10,000 that they couldn't. Once again, the race was on! This was one race Charles Crocker intended to win.

Central Pacific laborers worked quickly to set the record for most track laid in a single day.

Crocker had all the ties and rails delivered to the exact spots where they would be used. At dawn on April 28, 1869, when the work whistle blew, 4,000 men rushed to their posts. They worked feverishly for the rest of the day. As soon as the ties were in place, another group laid the track, then another crew pounded in the spikes.

The Central Pacific crew finished the day with 10 miles (16.1 km) and 56 feet (17.1 m) in place. In 12 hours, they had set 3,520 rails and 25,800 ties. Crocker's crew not only set a record, they also made sure it would hold. The Union Pacific had less than 9 miles (14.5 km) left to go, so they couldn't possibly break the record.

sabotage—damage or destruction of property that is done on purpose

CHAPTER 5

PROMONTORY SUMMIT AND THE GOLDEN SPIKE

By May 1869, the two railroads had been inching toward each other for years. It was decided that Promontory Summit, Utah, would be the place where the tracks came together. It was 1,086 miles (1,748 km) from Omaha, and 690 miles (1,110 km) from Sacramento. The end was almost in sight.

But when the two companies were almost within shouting distance of each other, something went wrong. Durant was traveling to Promontory Summit for the special "Golden Spike Ceremony" to unite the two railroads. But on May 6, the train stopped so suddenly that passengers fell to the floor. A mob of angry Union Pacific laborers boarded the train and took Durant hostage. They had not been paid for three months, and there would be no ceremony until they received their wages! Durant sent a telegram to chief engineer Dodge and arranged payment. Forty-eight hours later, the money arrived, and Durant was released.

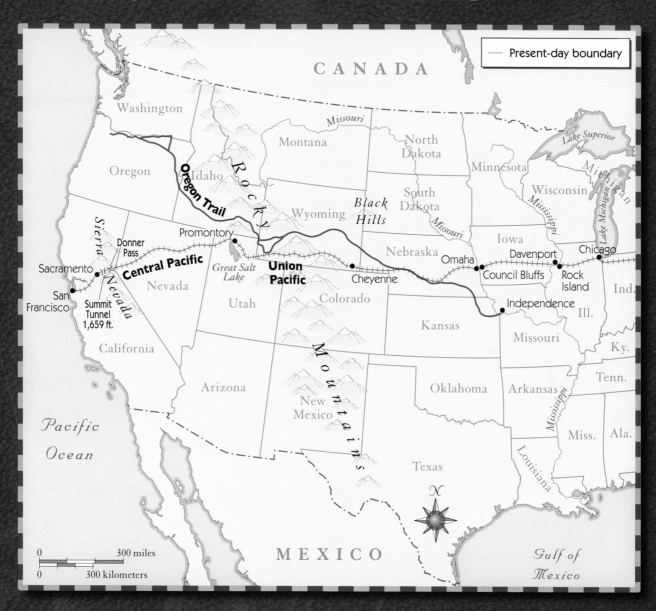

Present-day boundary

CANADA

Washington

Oregon

Idaho

Montana

Missouri

North Dakota

Minnesota

Wisconsin

Lake Superior

Lake Michigan

South Dakota

Wyoming

Black Hills

Rocky

Oregon Trail

Sierra

Nevada

Donner Pass

Promontory

Central Pacific

Great Salt Lake

Union Pacific

Cheyenne

Nebraska

Omaha

Council Bluffs

Davenport

Rock Island

Chicago

Iowa

Mississippi

Sacramento

San Francisco

Summit Tunnel 1,659 ft.

Nevada

Utah

Colorado

Kansas

Independence

Missouri

Ind.

Ill.

Ky.

California

Arizona

New Mexico

Mountains

Oklahoma

Arkansas

Tenn.

Miss.

Ala.

Pacific Ocean

Louisiana

Texas

N

Mississippi

MEXICO

Gulf of Mexico

0   300 miles

0   300 kilometers

Representatives from the Union Pacific and Central Pacific took turns tapping the final spike of the first transcontinental railroad in place.

Hitting the Nail on the Head—Or Not

Finally on May 10, 1869, the ceremony began. The Central Pacific's engine *Jupiter* met the Union Pacific's *Engine 119*. In addition to the golden spike, there was also a silver spike from Nevada, one of gold and silver from Arizona, and an iron spike from Colorado.

The Golden Spike

To add to the excitement, the entire country would get the news at the same time. A telegraph operator was in position to tap out the announcement that the final spike was in place. Representing the Central Pacific, Stanford raised a silver-plated hammer, took a mighty swing, … and missed. Durant took the hammer and swung it hard for the Union Pacific. He missed too! The crowd laughed. Stanford and Durant might have been rich and powerful businessmen, but neither one could pound a nail.

The hammer was then passed around and several men, including Grenville Dodge and James Strobridge, each gave it a light tap. But it was Hanna Strobridge who gave it the final tap.

At 12:47 p.m., when the Golden Spike was in place, the telegraph operator tapped out, "Done!" All across the country, parades were held and cannons were fired. As one telegram read, "The iron wedding is … accomplished." Indeed, "Miss Atlantic" had just married "Mr. Pacific."

From Sea to Shining Sea

In the end, the first transcontinental railroad met its goal. Other transcontinental railroads to the north and south soon followed, and together they opened up the West. Towns flourished along the railroad route. Manufacturers easily moved their goods to far-flung places. Cattlemen built ranches. What was once open prairie became farms growing wheat and corn to feed America's growing population.

Immigrants found unlimited opportunities out west. More women and children arrived too. As a result came schools, churches, music, and theater, all of which helped tame the Wild West. In 1890 the U.S. census noted that the American frontier had disappeared. The new railroad provided a faster, easier, and cheaper way to travel, so the once-important Oregon Trail was seldom used.

∾ FUN FACT ∾

The transcontinental railroad dropped the cost of traveling cross-country from nearly $1,000 to $150 per person.

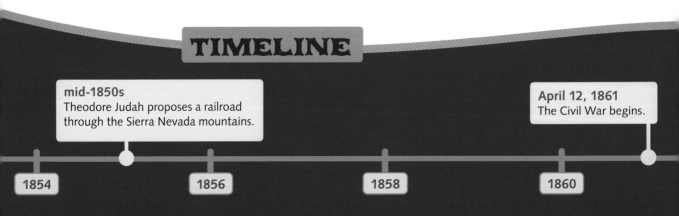

TIMELINE

mid-1850s
Theodore Judah proposes a railroad through the Sierra Nevada mountains.

April 12, 1861
The Civil War begins.

1854 — 1856 — 1858 — 1860

But not everyone benefited. In fact, American Indians suffered greatly. Their former hunting grounds were taken over by settlers and their treasured buffalo became nearly extinct as hunters killed the animals for sport. Eventually, the American Indians were forced to live on **reservations**.

In the end, the Chinese, Irish, and everyone else who labored on the transcontinental railroad earned a heroic place in history. Their backbreaking work created an engineering feat that many had thought impossible. Best of all, it took only a week to ride the rails from sea to shining sea.

reservation—an area of land set aside by the U.S. government for American Indians

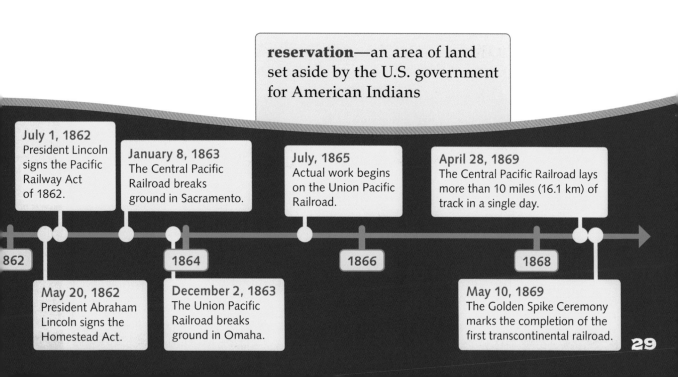

July 1, 1862
President Lincoln signs the Pacific Railway Act of 1862.

January 8, 1863
The Central Pacific Railroad breaks ground in Sacramento.

July, 1865
Actual work begins on the Union Pacific Railroad.

April 28, 1869
The Central Pacific Railroad lays more than 10 miles (16.1 km) of track in a single day.

862

1864

1866

1868

May 20, 1862
President Abraham Lincoln signs the Homestead Act.

December 2, 1863
The Union Pacific Railroad breaks ground in Omaha.

May 10, 1869
The Golden Spike Ceremony marks the completion of the first transcontinental railroad.

GLOSSARY

bond (BAHND)—a paper that shows a person has loaned money to a company or government and will receive a larger amount in return

handcar (HAND-kar)—a small, four-wheeled railroad car operated by hand

immigrant (IM-uh-gruhnt)—a person who moves from one country to live permanently in another

isthmus (ISS-muhss)—a narrow strip of land that has water on both sides and connects two larger sections of land

Louisiana Purchase (loo-ee-zee-AN-uh PURchuhss)—an 1803 deal with France in which the United States bought land that would eventually become parts of 15 states

malaria (muh-LAIR-ee-ah)—a serious disease that people get from mosquito bites; malaria causes high fever, chills, and sometimes death

railroad tie (RAYL-rohd TYE)—a rectangular, wooden support for the rails in railroad tracks

reservation (rez-er-VAY-shuhn)—an area of land set aside by the U.S. government for American Indians

sabotage (SAB-uh-tahzh)—damage or destruction of property that is done on purpose

secede (si-SEED)—to formally withdraw from a group or an organization, often to form another organization

trestle (TRESS-uhl)—a framework that holds up a railroad bridge

yellow fever (YEL-oh FEE-vur)—an illness that can cause high fever, chills, nausea, kidney and liver failure; liver failure causes the skin to become yellow, giving the disease its name

READ MORE

Bailer, Darice. *The Last Rail.* Smithsonian Odyssey Adventure. Norwalk, Conn.: Soundprints, 2011.

Perritano, John. *The Transcontinental Railroad.* A True Book. New York: Children's Press, 2010.

Sandler, Martin W. *Who Were the American Pioneers? And Other Questions About ... Westward Expansion.* Good Question! New York: Sterling Children's Books, 2014.

Thompson, Linda. *Building the Transcontinental Railroad.* History of America. Vero Beach, Fla.: Rourke Educational Media, 2013.

INTERNET SITES

FactHound offers a safe, fun way to find Internet sites related to this book. All of the sites on FactHound have been researched by our staff.

Here's all you do:

Visit *www.facthound.com*

Type in this code: 9781491401866

 **Super-cool stuff!** Check out projects, games and lots more at **www.capstonekids.com**

CRITICAL THINKING USING THE COMMON CORE

1. If you had lived during the mid-1800s, would you have liked to work on the transcontinental railroad? Would you have used it for travel or to move out west? Explain your answer. (Text Types and Purposes)

2. List at least three ways that the American Indians' opinion of the transcontinental railroad contrasted with the point of view of the white settlers. (Craft and Structure)

3. How did the completion of the transcontinental railroad lead to the end of the Oregon Trail? (Key Ideas and Details)

INDEX

DATE DUE

			PRINTED IN U.S.A.